TH
TRUTH
ABOUT
BULLYING

THE ESSENTIAL GUIDE
FOR PARENTS & TEACHERS

NORRY ASCROFT

Cover Design by 100Covers.com
Interior Design by FormattedBooks.com

ISBN: 978-1-8380468-0-4 (Paperback)

Winner Publishing

CONTENTS

INTRODUCTION

"INSANITY: DOING THE same thing over and over again and expecting different results" Albert Einstein.

What you are about to read in this book is totally different than any other information on bullying that is available elsewhere, and it ***needs*** to be. After extensive research of the information that children, parents, and teachers are currently getting, it is no surprise to me that we are not making a big enough difference with the problem of bullying.

There are many websites and organisations doing great work highlighting what bullying is, and bringing massive awareness of the problem, with some of them giving sound *logical* examples of ways to help.

I am certainly in no way criticising any of them, as they are helping to make a difference. But it is no way near a big enough difference. The Truth About Bullying is not meant to replace other information and programs on bullying, it is meant to give you the foundations of the problem and help what is already being done.

Unfortunately, all forms of bullying are increasing at an alarming rate. That is just a fact, and something different must be done. The information in this book is different and it does make a direct difference.

So why hasn't bullying ended, when so many of these organisations have pledged to do it? It's because bullying is a 'Human Behaviour Weakness' which is controlled by our *emotions* not just logic.

You see logically there is no need to bully someone, and logically it should not hurt our feelings. Do you remember the saying 'sticks & stones may break my bones, but names can never hurt me'?

Well every child and adult who has been bullied will disagree. I know this because I have asked every one of those that I have helped over the years and guess what.... they disagree.

They feel hurt, with many of them holding onto that pain for a long time, well after the bullying has ended. It is logically true that names can never hurt you, but it must be explained differently than is being done so far, for it to ***feel*** true.

We tell children who have been physically bullied that the bully is weak and a coward. This is totally true and *logically* correct, but the victim certainly doesn't agree. I know because, once again, I have asked many victims.

The physically bullied child has a fear from their experience, that convinces them that the bully is tough, strong, and a constant threat. What is even worse is that the bullies themselves think they are tough and strong, and they will have justified to themselves why they did what they did.

If it were just down to logic, we wouldn't have the need for this book or any other help, but logic is only one part of the understanding of bullying and ultimately our *emotions* are in control.

Even though I never suffered from bullying myself, I became emotionally involved with helping children and adults with bullying & mental health issues. You would think that it doesn't make sense for me logically to care so much, but hey that's emotions for you.

Let me explain to you why I got involved in helping with the bullying problem and why I am so passionate to help, because it certainly wasn't part of my goals and life plans back in 2008.

Back then. I was doing company presentations and trainings for an organisation, which gave me the opportunity to fly to Chicago for a seminar with America's No.1 Success Coach, Jack Canfield. I wanted to take his yearlong training—Train The Trainer—which was a big commitment.

My plan was to expand and grow the personal and corporate trainings that I was doing, as well as speaking engagements, which was the logical thing to do for my career.

The only thing that I did not count on was for my emotions to overrule my logic and change everything. This is what happened.

Whilst waiting in the airport for that flight to Chicago I was reading a newspaper, and it had an article about a teenage girl who had died by suicide, because of cyberbullying.

This was the third story of a teenage suicide in as many weeks that I had read, all of them because of the effects of bullying. I can't explain in words how it 'hit' me, but all I can say is that every time I think of, or share her story, it makes my eyes fill up and I feel like crying.

Even writing about it right now makes me emotional and I am not ashamed to admit it. That is the power of our emotions.

Maybe it's because I'm a parent myself, I don't know. But what I do know is that these stories gave me an awful feeling. This feeling was the motivator for me to research into what was being done about combating bullying.

You see, with all the learning and training that I had done on human behaviour and personal development, I knew straight away the truth behind the bullying.

All of the information I found online was very similar and not explaining anywhere near enough what is needed to make a real difference for the victims of bullying, or even to help the bullies themselves understand, and hopefully stop their weak behaviour.

I couldn't understand why nobody was going deeper and clearer with such an important issue, and I remember it making me feel even more upset for that teenage girl and all her family and friends.

If she, and the thousands of other kids who have taken their own lives, had better education on this subject, then maybe they would have been strong enough to get through the bullying and still be with us today.

Maybe her bullies would have understood how weak and selfish they were being and not carried on with their horrible behaviour.

As I say, it wasn't *logic* that got me so passionate about helping with bullying, it was an *emotional* decision and it really got to me.

Any of my family or friends will vouch that it has become an obsessive subject for me, and I probably talk about it too much. I don't apologise for this, because bullying is too serious to ignore. I do however thank them for their understanding and continuous support.

It is not acceptable to say that bullying is just part of growing up and that you just have to *toughen up*. Not when it is happening on a totally unprecedented scale due to the internet, social media, mobile phones etc. There is no safe escape for some of our kids.

It can also cause all kinds of mental health problems and at the very least will hold our next generation back from reaching their true potential, because bullying causes lower self-esteem and lower confidence.

I'm probably one of the most positive people you could meet, but let me tell you the first TRUTH of bullying..... it will never stop!

Now do not be alarmed or downhearted, or think that I'm being defeatist or negative. I am just being truthful. Because as long as there are humans, there will be weak human behaviours.

Even if every single human being on the planet reads this book, there will still be a small amount of bullies. Why? Because it is an easy, selfish, and weak way to get our *emotional needs* (I will be explaining these 'Needs' later, in detail).

With that said, I am positive that we can dramatically reduce bullying, and more than certain that anyone being bullied can win against it and not remain a victim.

There will always be some people who demonstrate 'Human Behaviour Weakness', so we have to educate children, as well as train parents & teachers about the truth behind bullying. That is what this book will do for you.

Let me tell you the second TRUTH about bullying (this one gets the biggest reactions)... bullying is NEVER personal.

Now before you start shouting and cursing, or throw this book across the room, please hear me out. I have shared this information with a few thousand kids, parents, and teachers, and most of them do not believe me at first that it's never personal.

But when they truly understand the truth about bullying and 'get it' (both emotionally and logically), it's just like magic. When the 'lightbulb' or 'aha' moment comes and they truly know and *feel* that it was never personal, that's when things change for them is such a positive way.

Read the whole book to the end, and if you still feel like shouting at me then you are more than welcome to rant away. But remember I know your rant will not be *personal* because I do this human behaviour work every day!

This book will provide you with a good understanding of what is really going on with bullying, and more importantly, how anyone can overcome the hurt and emotional pain it causes.

I am going to keep it as simple as I can in the book, but like anything new it may take you a couple of times of reading for you to get the full benefit.

If you have experienced any form of bullying, you will find this information enlightening, and a way to release and let go of the past hurt and pain.

You may be a parent whose child is/has been bullied and is looking for some help in dealing with it. Maybe you are a teacher who wants to make a direct difference to your class and school.

I truly believe that this book can help you to really understand bullying to a level that you can't be emotionally hurt ever again by anyone.

As soon as you start reading, you may find that certain hurts and upsets from bullying start to disappear at an unconscious level. This has happened many times to other people just from reading this information.

The memory of the bullying event does not cause any painful feelings anymore, because you will truly know the human behaviour weakness behind any kind of bullying.

I believe that prevention is better than cure. And if we could teach this to school children at an early age, what a difference it would make to their mental health and self-esteem.

The information you are about to read is all based on human behaviour, so it can be filtered into any activities that your children are doing, and at any age.

Parents and teachers can be creative in the ways they do this based on the knowledge of the children you look after. I will be sharing with you a few examples of how to do this for different age groups.

The statistics for bullying and mental health are alarming. You only have to go to any bullying website to see the figures and proof, which can make you feel like it's a lost cause, or something that we can't change and is inevitable.

Well it is not. We can all do something about it, and it starts right now with you reading this book. We cannot control the bully's behaviour, but we can control our own response towards them. This will help by putting ourselves in the position of power, rather than giving it to those weak individuals who bully.

I hope one day this information I am about to share with you will be taught to every child in every school. Drip fed, on a daily basis, so that it becomes as easy and natural to them as 2+2=4.

It will build their self-esteem, their confidence, and their resilience to a high level, and ultimately help them to have strong and positive mental health.

For now, it is up to us as individual parents and teachers to share with our youth and help them reach their true potential.

The first way to win against bullying is to truly understand it. Then we are in a stronger position to deal with it.

Let's get into chapter one now, so we can get to the bottom of what's really going on with bullying. We start with the con-trick.

CHAPTER ONE

THE MAGIC TRICK & THE CON-TRICK

DO YOU LIKE magic tricks? I do.

I have always loved them since I was a kid, amazed at the skill and entertainment from the people who perform them.

Have you, just like me, wanted to know how the trick was done? Are you curious to see exactly what is really going on?

Part of you wants to know how it is done, and part of you doesn't want to know how they do it. You see, once you know how a trick is done, the trick can never be the same. The revealed illusion cannot be undone.

The great thing about good magic tricks is that it is a win-win for everyone. The person performing the trick for entertainment feels good, and the person or audience watching the trick feel good too. A true win-win.

Now, have you ever seen or heard of a con-trick, where people lose their money? You know, like the three cups and pea trick. This is where they hide the pea under one of the cups, move the cups around, and you bet your money and guess which cup it is under.

This has been an old favourite on the streets of any city around the world, and unbelievably people still fall for this con-trick today and lose their money.

There are many different versions of this classic con with playing cards too, but the result is just the same… you lose your money because it is a pure con-trick.

A true win-lose, in favour of the con artist. You cannot, and never will win, and you definitely want to know how these con-tricks are done.

The interesting thing (and the point I want you to understand) is that the fundamentals for the good magic trick and the bad con-trick are the same. They both require the same principles and skills to deflect you away from what is really going on.

Even though *logically* you know the 'con' is too good to be true, the manipulator works on you *emotionally* and pulls you in. The con –artist gives you a false sense of security and suddenly you are already picturing what you will be spending your winnings on.

You will have just seen someone else win before you (someone who is part of the con-team) and believe this will be easy winnings.

How many times do people you know get tricked and conned in real life situations, or controlled & manipulated in toxic or abusive relationships? You say to yourself "Why do they keep going back to that person who is treating them so bad, it doesn't make *logical* sense".

No, it does not make *logical* sense, because it's *emotionally* driven. More on this later.

Bullying is one of the biggest con-tricks of human behaviour. It is a pure con, a true win-lose in favour of the bully, and it is never personal (I know you still don't believe me yet, but you will).

Even if the bullies themselves feel it is personal towards their victim, it isn't.

The bullies do not even know the real truth of their weak actions and behaviour. And this is a major part of the problem that needs properly addressing.

Every time we interact with someone it should *logically* be a win-win, just like a good magic trick. Both people should find the experience pleasurable and leave with good feelings. Simple.

Unfortunately, we are human, and our unconscious *emotions* are involved, which we have never been taught about in school.

When you were growing up did you receive an owner's guide, or instruction manual for your feelings?

No? I didn't think so.

We just try and figure it out for ourselves, based on our life experiences and hope for the best. We do our utmost to avoid any painful feelings and hope to gain some pleasurable feelings along the way.

Some of us turn out ok, and some unfortunately do not. Well that is just not good enough anymore for our children, and we must do something about it. It is just not worth the gamble.

The good magic trick and the bad con trick are fundamentally the same, they deflect you away from what is really going on. The only difference is the *person* who is performing the trick. And the same goes for bullying.

We are all humans looking to get our daily *emotional needs*, and we will get them in a good or bad way.

Something I do in presentations, or family sessions, is show kids a mind trick. I make out that I am going to influence them with my magical and powerful mind influencing talent. The trick has already started because I am giving them suggestions verbally to distract their conscious mind away from what is really going on.

It doesn't matter what I say to them, it's just a distraction. Remember this for later because the same applies to the bully.

I do not actually have any mystical or mind reading skills. The truth is a friend of mine, Simon, showed me how to do this easy trick.

I persuaded him to reveal the simple technique to me so I could use it as an example to help kids (that sentence is just in case he gets in trouble with magicians for giving out secrets!).

After Simon showed me how he did it, I could not believe how simple and obvious the trick was. I was convinced that if I tried it on anyone, they wouldn't fall for it and I would be busted.

Guess what? In all the times I've shared it, nobody has seen the truth behind it, and they're always shocked to see how easy and simple it really is (this is what we want everyone to feel when they really understand the bullying con).

Once I have shown them how the trick is done, I then say "let me do the trick again and this time you will bet with your money"

The reply is always a big NO, and rightly so. They now know there is no chance of winning and they will lose their money. Once you know how a trick is done you cannot be conned by the same trick ever again.

Bullying is a con-trick and we are going to reveal the secret truths and expose bullying for what it really is.

TOP TIP

You can learn simple tricks on YouTube. Just type in–How To Do Magic Tricks or Mind Tricks.

As a parent it is a great way of starting the bullying conversation with your child and to demonstrate the difference between good magic tricks and bad con-tricks.

Kids find it fun and it will help you then progress into sharing the other information you will learn in this book.

Teachers can include the whole class, just as I have done in schools, and even in assemblies. I always explain that now everyone in the class, or the year group, and even the whole school now knows how the trick is done, I cannot con any of them again.

If I keep trying the con-trick on them it will be a waste of time and most likely end in embarrassment for me, as the other kid's just laugh at my weak behaviour.

This is what we want to happen with the bullies. When every child and teacher in school knows the con-trick of bullying then the bully cannot get their emotional needs in a bad way. The bully ends up just looking foolish as nobody is giving them the responses they are craving for.

The bully will know the real reason why they are doing it, and this will have a better chance of the bully *changing* their behaviour themselves.

Everyone in a class knows for certain that 2+2=4. It is undeniable and fixed. If I start shouting at people saying 2+2=5, nobody will feel hurt or upset.

More than likely everyone in the class will look at each other and just think I am crazy or know that I am acting up for attention because of my own weak and selfish reasons.

When the whole class/school knows with certainty the con-trick of bullying, then the weak behaviour of the bully cannot, and will not, hurt them *emotionally*.

Whether it is physical, verbal, or cyber bullying, the con-trick is the same. The bully is *using* their victim for their own selfish *emotional needs*.

The only difference between a bully and the con-artist, who tricks people for money, is that the bully is stealing something more valuable than money. They are robbing our kids of their self-esteem & confidence.

This is truly why bullies are weak. Because strong people don't have to attack others physically or verbally for the sake of their own selfish needs. Am I getting too deep yet?

You now know that bullying is a con-trick and I want you to use your brilliant imagination to picture this con-trick example throughout the book.

You don't have to become a psychologist or a trained therapist to understand and use this information. I have plenty of friends and associates in both these professions who will vouch for that.

However, you do have to read the whole book, for it to all fit into place.

Just think of it as… read it till you feel it !

Sorry for that statement. When I said it in my mind it sounded cool. I will ask the editor to delete it and try to shake off my embarrassment

Anyway, let's get started in the next chapter and see how our subconscious friend is going to help us against the bullying con.

CHAPTER TWO

OUR SUBCONSCIOUS FRIEND

THIS WILL AMAZE you.

When I got out of bed this morning, I stood up without even thinking how to do it. I just did it. I then walked to the bathroom, moving my legs one after the other without thinking how to do it. I just walked, and I can't even tell you which leg went first, the left or the right.

Amazing, I know.

In the bathroom I then brushed my teeth whilst not concentrating on which hand I was using. I just brushed away whilst I was consciously thinking of what I had planned for the day. Amazing, I know.

Ok, it's not so amazing, and I'll stop giving anymore silly examples.

We have all done these same actions for so many years that we don't have to think or question how to do them.

We could share endless examples of things that at first, we really had to concentrate and think about doing, and now we just do automatically, all thanks to our subconscious friend.

I am not going to give you all the fancy psychological details of the subconscious mind right now, although I am tempted to impress you with my knowledge and expertise (remember this ego statement for chapter 4).

For the moment I want you to use your great imagination again to think of your subconscious as being your minds hard drive, like a computer.

All your memories and emotions stored as data in that part of your supercomputer mind. Told you it's amazing.

Have you visualised it? Good.

We are going to start uploading brilliant information about bullying and human behaviour to your supercomputer mind. And just like every other thing you have repeated into a habit, it will then get transferred into your subconscious.

Once that is completed then it is happy days.

Just like walking, tying your shoelaces, picking up a cup, etc, you will just automatically know the truth about the bullying, and you will know with certainty that it is never personal (getting closer to this truth. I promise).

Can I share a personal story? Picture this.

A few years ago, I was driving my car with my daughter in the passenger seat, who at the time was only about 10yrs old. She was mildly annoyed with something going on in her 'world', so I decided to do a little 'pattern interrupt' technique on her.

I interrupted her negative downloading (I made that term up for moaning), by abruptly telling her to answer this question as quickly as she possibly could. "What is two plus two?"

In a split second, my daughter had answered with the correct answer of four. I had successfully taken her thoughts away from the circumstances in her 'world' by answering this very simple question.

I then quickly asked her "How do you know it's four?"

She gave me that look! The one that indicates without words "Realllllly. Are you serious?"

Every parent knows what look I mean.

Her highly toned vocal reply was "Daaaad. Everyone knows that 2+2=4".

To have some fun (a dad's duty is to wind up their kids) I then asked her if she was absolutely sure, and certain that the answer was four.

This question got me an even more scrunched up face from her than before.

I then proceeded to ask her if she had pictured or imagined two apples + two apples = four apples, in her mind, when I asked the question.

Now she was ready to flip out, and said quite loudly "Why would I do that?"

I then explained to her that when she was very young, I used to read her a book that taught with shiny pictures of how 2 apples + 2 apples = 4 apples. Then after enough repetition and understanding, she did not need the shiny apples, and it just became 2+2=4.

If I ask her the same math question now, her brain just pops up with the correct answer of four in a split second.

She heard the 2+2 from me (auditory) and didn't even have to picture (visual) or imagine 2+2, because her subconscious mind just knew (from the auditory of my voice) with 100% certainty and provided the correct answer for her.

All done in a split second.

I could get into all the conscious, subconscious, unconscious mind details for you, but you don't really need it.

Remember what I told you. You don't have to become a psychologist or therapist.

So how does this story relate to you and the kids we want to help?

Well, imagine this new information on bullying being like the 2 apples + 2 apples example. Like anything in life, the more you repeat and understand, the easier it gets.

Pretty soon, just as you don't need to picture shiny apples for this equation, your subconscious friend will already be skipping past your self-talk that says "Why is the bully doing this? I need to know exactly the reason why".

You won't need to know the exact reason, because it won't matter too you. It is *their* human behaviour weakness and it is not your problem.

You would never find out the precise reason anyway because the bully themselves don't really know.

When you are consistently using this information in your daily life, you will get to the stage in which your subconscious friend quickly rejects with certainty, what the con-artist bully says or does. Just in the same way it does with the correct answer of 4 in the math question.

This will then put you in a better state to respond and deal with any bullying. The first stage is to truly understand the truth about bullying.

So far so good.

Here is a quick update for your supercomputer brain. Let these truths sink in.

- Bullying is a con-trick.
- The Bully is only using you to get their 'fix' of *emotional* needs.
- It is ***not*** personal and never was (you will believe me)
- Your Subconscious Friend is going to make this as simple as 2+2=4.
- When you thought of the apples, you imagined them being red ones (I'm just messing with you with this one)

Here we go. The Truth About Bullying. Four parts to the foundation of human behaviour.

I want you to visualise in your mind a table. Imagine the tabletop as the bullying problem and it is all you can see. You (and others) are trying to bash/break the tabletop with your fists, which is not working because the tabletop is being firmly held up by the four strong legs hidden underneath—out of sight.

The quickest and easiest way to collapse the tabletop (bullying problem), is to focus your energy on the legs (human behaviour). Once you take away the legs, any tabletop (problem) will collapse, no matter how strong.

No time to waste. Let's get started on the next chapter with Table Leg 1.

CHAPTER THREE

OUR MODEL OF THE WORLD – LEG 1

OK, HERE GOES, a quick explanation of the first part of the human behaviour foundation that I use. One of the four legs.

You, me, them, everybody… sounds like the intro to the Blues Brothers song!

We ALL have over 50'000 thoughts every day. Wow!

When I first heard that, I was training with Jack Canfield in San Diego and it just blew me away. It also gave me a few more thoughts to think about!

I have since researched different neuroscience reports and studies, that put the figure to be anything between 60-90 thousand thoughts.

We don't need to know the exact amount so let's just keep it simple and stick to the over 50k figure.

The main fact to realise is that we are basically a thought factory. We are thinking all day—every day.

Most of these thoughts are naturally about ourselves and our circumstances. And believe it or not they are more negative than positive. We tend to self-criticise and judge ourselves with our self-talk and inner dialogue. We also tend to focus more on what we don't want than what we do want. It's perfectly normal by the way, we are just trying to stay safe and certain (more on this later).

Don't get yourself down though, it's not all negative, we do have thousands of positive thoughts too.

Every single one of these thoughts creates a feeling/emotion inside us. Happy or sad, pleasure or pain, feeling good or bad about ourselves etc.

These feelings and emotions then influence our behaviour and drive forward our actions. Pretty simple so far?

What's this got to do with bullying I hear you ask? Be patient young Jedi, this is all part of your Yoda training and will all make sense.

You don't need to know all about the different parts of the brain, mind and thought process, or the chemical names of stuff running around your body.

Remember what I said.... you don't have to become a psychologist or therapist. Your subconscious friend is cool with this by the way.

All you need to know is this simple formula in the order of...

THOUGHTS > EMOTIONS > BEHAVIOUR

When it comes to bullying, most people focus on the bullies' behaviour.

This is normal because of the hurt and pain that this awful action has caused. But their behaviour is just a clue to what is really going on.

Think of our con-trick example for a moment. The behaviour/action of the trickster is to divert and deflect your attention away from the truth.

When the bully hurts your feelings and puts you in a 'state' of upset or anger, they have successfully got you where they want you. They have deflected you away from the *truth* of their weak human behaviour.

When I help adult clients with any emotional issues, I call this part the 'story'. They have a story of what has happened, or is still happening, based on other people's behaviour and actions.

I listen to the 'story', but I am already searching for their thoughts and emotions behind it. This is what you will do when understanding a bully.

You see, the bully is having thousands of thoughts just like you. Their thoughts also create emotions and feelings just like you, and it is these thoughts and emotions that are driving them to act in a cruel and weak manner.

The bully has put themselves in a negative or bad 'state' and it will be based on *their* circumstances and experiences in life. It has nothing to do with you, and if you were not there, the bully would just use someone else.

The bullies do not truly know why they do it, so they never take 100% responsibility for their weak actions.

A bully will never feel truly fulfilled in life and therefore if they don't change their behaviour, they will live a life unfulfilled and frustrated. Unfortunately, this is why many bullies never change.

When we think our thoughts, then feel our feelings and emotions, we put ourselves into a 'state'. Now that can be a good or bad–positive or negative 'state'.

Happy or Sad – Pleasure or Pain

The 'state' that we put ourselves in is a choice, and it is OUR choice. The bully has created their own 'state' too.

You now know that we are having over 50'000 thoughts a day. We are using these thoughts to either build up good beliefs or bad beliefs of ourselves, and of others, and everything that affects us.

Remember....

OUR THOUGHTS create EMOTIONS & FEELINGS that create our ACTIONS & BEHAVIOUR.

Now this is important.

We are NOT our behaviour... Everyone has done silly or stupid things, and maybe said bad things we didn't really mean. We are not stupid or mean people; we were just in a bad/negative 'state' at the time because of bad/negative thoughts and feelings.

Sometimes we allow our 'state' to be created by what others have said or done to us, or things which are out of our control. When this happens, we are letting others affect our thinking, our feelings, and our behaviour.

The truth is, we can all take control of these things.

Unfortunately, the bullies do not take responsibility for their own thoughts and emotions and use the selfish and weak behaviour of attacking others, either verbally or physically.

When you realise what the bully is actually doing, then you start to truly understand the con-trick.

Understanding the truth behind bullying is the first step and then you are stronger to deal with it.

Top Tip

If someone has done something wrong and you are 'telling them off', then make sure that person knows that it is their behaviour that is being criticised and not them personally.

If you tell me off and I take it personally, then my emotions will kick in and my defence mode will be activated. I will try and justify my bad behaviour and even try to switch the blame in any way I can.

I will probably convince myself that I am being unfairly judged and misunderstood, and act like I am now the victim.

This happens all the time in relationships, the workplace, and of course bullying. It is a human behaviour weakness because we all must try and protect our feelings.

It takes courage and strength to accept responsibility, but unfortunately, it is easier not to. This is one reason that makes bullies weak.

If you explain clearly to me that you are actually criticising my behaviour and not me personally, I will be more receptive to listen with my defence mode lowered.

Show me how I acted weak, in the negative 'state' which ***I*** had created, then I am more likely to take responsibility for my actions.

You encourage me to be stronger and better in the future with my behaviour because my bad behaviour just shows me as weak and selfish.

There are consequences and punishment for my bad behaviour, but it is not personal, so I may be in a better state to accept it and understand.

More importantly, if done right, I will be better informed now and feel like changing my future behaviour. I will also have no excuses if I don't take responsibility to change my behaviour.

I will be in no position to claim to be 'hard done to' or being 'set an example of'.

There will be more explanation in detail later in the book. For now, read this next important piece of our human behaviour jigsaw.

Our 'Model' Of The World

How old are you?

It is ok if you don't want to divulge that information, I understand. I am a bit shy about sharing my age too, but at the time of writing this book I am fortyish.

Ok, I am actually forty-nine. There, you got it out of me.

That means that I have had forty-nine years of thoughts, emotions, and behaviours, based on my circumstances and experiences in my life. This all culminates to my beliefs and views of myself, and the world at this present time.

In trainings and therapy, I use the term for this as 'Model of the World'.

I have my model of the world, which is called Norry's model (because that is my name), and you have your model of the world. Please use your own name for this!

Now, in my model of the world coffee is better than tea. sweet & sour chicken is the best Chinese meal, and Scooby Doo are the best cartoons ever.

A lot of my beliefs and opinions have changed over the years (just like yours have) based on the information and experiences I have had in my life.

Just for the sake of this example, I want you to imagine that in your model of the world, you think tea is better than coffee.

You also believe that chow mein is a tastier Chinese meal than my sweet & sour. You also have the crazy thoughts that Tom & Jerry is better than Scooby Doo (to be fair it is a close call).

Now we have Norry's model of the world, and your model of the world. Whose model is right? Whose model is wrong?

The answer is neither. We are not right or wrong, because it is just our model of our world. Let me first explain where I am going with this by using a phobia example.

When we are born we only have two fears. The fear of falling, and the fear of sudden loud noises. Everything else we become scared of in our lives is ***created.***

Fears like spiders, snakes, flying etc. These fears are created by us, but they are not real.

Now, I know phobia fears are very real to the person with them, but it is not the TRUTH.

Let us use spiders for this example. I am not going into the psychology or cures for phobias here, it's just to make my point.

Some people are scared of spiders and some people are not. There are many people who not only like spiders, but actually love them as pets. They even let big hairy spiders crawl over them! FACT.

So, if being scared of spiders (or having a full-on panic attack inducing phobia) was the TRUTH, then every single person on the planet would be scared of them.

We would all have to feel the same way for it to be an undisputed TRUTH.

Have you got it? If not, read again before we get back to my coffee and love of Scooby Doo.

In Norry's model of the world I believe that my coffee is better than your tea. But it is not the TRUTH. It is just my belief, preference and opinion, based on my life experience so far. There is no best drink and that is the TRUTH.

Coffee and tea are just drinks, and that is it.

There is no best Chinese meal or cartoon either. You believe the best is the one in your model of the world, but it is not the TRUTH.

My sweet & sour is just food, and Scooby Doo is just a cartoon.

I actually felt massive resistance saying Scooby Doo is just a cartoon! Please don't judge me.

From this, I want you to understand that the bully has their model of their world. Quite often the school bully will have a go at someone simply because of a difference of beliefs or opinions, taste in clothes, music, football team, intelligence, religion, sexuality etc.

The list is endless, and it is never personal because it is just based on the bully's model of the world. They are weak and feel like they must prove their beliefs are right by attacking or making ridicule of your beliefs.

Now, I am allowed to think and feel that my coffee is better than your tea, but that doesn't give me the right to attack and bully you about it.

If I did, then in truth, I would only be using you to make me feel certain about my beliefs in my model of the world.

That is one reason why bullying is a human behaviour weakness, and why bullying is never personal.

Some mind notes for your conscious and subconscious friends.

- We are a thought factory with over 50'000 thoughts a day
- It is our thoughts that create our feelings & emotions
- These emotions drive our behaviour
- We are not our behaviour, but simply in a temporary 'state'
- The bully is truly weak because they are not controlling their thoughts and emotions in a good way
- We all have our own 'Model' of the world, based on our beliefs.
- The behaviour of the bully is the deflection part of the con-trick
- Weak people don't take responsibility for their bad behaviour

You have already learnt more about the human behaviour weakness behind bullying than you will anywhere else, but this is where it goes to a level higher.

The next chapter is all about our ***emotional needs*** and is going to expose the bullying con-trick for what it really is.

This is the part I love sharing with parents, teachers, and kids. It gets to the TRUTH of what is really going on.

Clear your mind and let your conscious and subconscious work together as a team. You are doing great.

p.s. I still like you even if you don't like Scooby Doo. I am strong enough to understand and respect your model of the world. It will not affect our friendship.

CHAPTER FOUR

OUR EMOTIONAL NEEDS – LEG 2

I AM PRESUMING you already know your *physical needs* in life.

Things like oxygen (you know that air stuff). I think you will agree that oxygen is pretty important to our *physical needs,* because without it we would die.

We also need food and water, and other essentials to survive physically. These are all ***needs***, not wants.

We don't just want oxygen; we desperately rely on it and ***need*** it to survive.

We know all this, and we even get some further education on our *physical needs* in certain school subjects.

What we don't get enough information on is something called our *Emotional Needs.*

Our ***Emotional Needs*** can be explained with different models from psychology and human behaviour experts. One of the first models I learnt almost thirty years ago is Maslow's Hierarchy of Needs.

This is a five-tier model that covers both physical and emotion needs and has been developed further since Maslow first released it in the 1940's.

I love Maslow's model and I know it is still being used widely in company trainings, but it is not the one I use in my trainings or with private clients. I use a simpler model first, before sharing Maslow's version.

It is still worth checking out after reading this in case you find it better in your model of the world.

What I am going to share with you in this chapter is a small version of what is called Primary Human Needs, or Primal Human Needs.

There are a couple of versions that teach nine Human Needs which we must get in life to survive *emotionally* and feel fulfilled.

In my experience, the simplest and best version (in Norry's model of the world) is by Tony Robbins & Chloe Madanes.

Tony has a model called The Six Human Needs which he has used and taught for decades, achieving outstanding results. If you would like to learn all of these *needs* in more detail, you can google Robbins Madanes Training/Strategic Intervention.

I have personally studied and trained in Strategic Intervention as part of my own ongoing learning and development. It has been one of the major tools that I use in trainings, therapy, and coaching.

What I did a few years ago in my work, was to change the name of Human Needs to Emotional Needs.

I only did this because I found that it was easier, especially for children, to call them *emotional needs* when explaining bullying.

I love sharing this information because of the results it brings.

Here are four of the *Emotional Needs* we will be using to expose the bullying con-trick.

Safe & Secure

At a basic level we ***need*** to ***feel*** safe. This can be anything from the environment we live in or maybe feeling safe about our job. Tony Robbins explains this *need* as Certainty.

Maybe it is feeling certain about your capabilities at something or that your relationship is going to last. It applies to anything and everything in your life. When we don't feel safe and secure in a good way, then we will find this *emotional need* in a bad way.

In many circumstances the bully has problems we do not know about, and unconsciously they fill this need in a bad way by hurting others, physically or mentally.

Bullying is the weak and easy option in this case because it takes no personal growth and is a selfish act.

The bully is just using anyone to get their *emotional needs.*

The bully doesn't truly understand they have this need, so they *logically* come up with a justifiable excuse to why they do it. The bully will also try to control others to get this *need.* And this will all be based on their 'model of the world'.

Remember what I told you. It is not personal.

Excitement/Danger

The correct name for this ***emotional need*** in Strategic Intervention is Variety. But as we are using it for bullying, we will be calling it excitement and danger.

*I should also point out that if you have had trainings/coaching from me in the past, this *need* was always called *Uncertainty**

The name is not so important to you right now, but the meaning will be.

We all have a *need* for some excitement, to experience something that makes us feel good. We can get this *need* in so many good ways from little daily activities.

Even the simple things like watching a new movie or going to watch a favourite band brings the feeling of variety and the unknown.

Have you ever wondered why someone would jump out of a plane with just a parachute, thousands of feet up in the sky? It is their way of feeling excitement and danger.

How many times have you heard about kids who have caused trouble or damaged property, and when caught they say that they don't know why they did it?

They *logically* claim it was because they were bored, and it was something to do.

They may have been bored, but the TRUTH is they were filling this *emotional need* of excitement or danger in a bad way.

The bully will use anyone to fill this *need.* They can physically attack someone for the excitement and the uncertainty of what's going to happen.

The bully will verbally abuse someone just for fun to get this need. They will spread rumours on social media for the excitement and danger that it brings just to get this *need.*

The bully gets their uncertainty by seeing if they can get you angry or upset. Whichever reaction they get, they win, because the reaction has fed their *Emotional Need.*

Remember it is never personal, just selfish.

Important/Special

We all have an emotional *need* to feel important, special, unique etc. And just like the other *needs*, we will get this in a good or bad way.

In training's I use Strategic Interventions term of Significance

This is certainly one of the main *emotional needs* that is driving the bullies' behaviour.

Feeling more important and powerful over someone else is a human behaviour weakness that is seen in every situation in life.

From relationships, the workplace, politics, religion, the feeling and believing that you are more important/special/significant than others has had devastating results.

The bully is using you to feed this *need* in a bad way and they don't really know why. It just fills their *need* and the feelings it gives them.

If the bully gets you angry or upset, their *need* is met. The more they control you with fear, the more this *need* is fed, and it becomes addictive, like a drug.

The bully is being selfish, and it is never personal. If they don't get this *need* from you, they will get it from someone else.

They will try and con you with any information they have of you.

It is as pathetic as me bullying you because you don't drink coffee. I insult you, embarrass you, and question why you don't fit into my 'model of the world'.

It has nothing to do with coffee, it is purely to do with me using you, so that I feel more important.

While you are distracted with anger or upset (and maybe questioning your 'model of the world'), I am stealing your self-esteem & confidence for my own selfish gain.

Even if you like coffee, I will still bully you for any other reason, like how many sugars you take, or maybe the brand of coffee you drink.

Remember the con-trick. It is never personal, even if I try and make it so.

The truth is, I am just using you to get my feeling of importance or the power of control over you.

Swap coffee to anything you relate to and see how it works.

If you are better than the bully at something and they feel less important/significant, then the weak response is for them to attack you, verbally or physically.

If you are not good at something, then the bully will still use you to build up their feelings of superiority. The bully doesn't care, because they are weak. It is never personal.

It could be the colour of your skin, the music you like, your style of clothes, your gender, religion, or your sexuality.

What the bully uses is just the deflection part of their con-trick. If they can make it seem more personal, their con-trick has more effect.

As long as they get you upset or angry, then its job done, and this *emotional need* is met.

By the way, earlier in the book I mentioned that I was tempted to try and impress you with my knowledge and expertise (ego). This would have been to make me feel more significant.

Feeling Connected – Feeling Loved

We all have a *need* for love and connection, and once again if we do not get these in a good way, we will get them in a bad way.

The bully can still feel connection simply by upsetting or controlling you. They may even feel a false sense of love or admiration from you because you are too scared to end a relationship or friendship with them.

The bully may be using you, just to feel connection and love with their own friends. This is one of the reasons why friends of the bully will either join in with the bullying, encourage it, or simply stand by and let the bullying happen.

If someone's main emotional driver is love and connection, and they are too scared to lose it, they will allow their friends to bully others, even if they themselves do not want to.

This partly explains why some people are called 'sheep'.

There are other emotional needs involved but at this stage of your understanding, I feel these will be enough to get across any example.

Remember, you don't have to become a psychologist to truly understand the bullying con-trick.

Once your subconscious friend processes these needs, by stories, examples, and repetition, then you do not actually have to know what the bully is after.

You will just know that the bully is trying to get maybe one, two, or a combination of all their *emotional needs*, by using you.

You won't care what *needs* their after, because you now know it's their own weakness and their own problem.

You are now in a stronger mental state to deal with the bully, and you also know with certainty that it is never personal.

The bullying con-trick has been exposed for what it truly is–weak human behaviour.

In training's I spend a lot of time sharing examples of life, where people get these emotional needs met in good or bad ways.

One of the examples is to do with football supporters. How a true football fan and a hooligan both get the same *emotional needs* in different ways.

A good supporter gets some form of certainty from their club or team. They get variety/uncertainty or excitement from watching their team because they don't know for certain the outcome—the result.

They also feel a sense of significance because they are associated with their club, and they feel connected, even loved, with that team and fellow supporters.

All their needs met in one go, and what I believe to be a good way.

The hooligan also feels a sense of certainty. They feel safe and secure with their crew. They also feel excitement, variety, or uncertainty, wondering if they are going to have trouble with other supporters. They love the adrenalin rush it gives them.

They also feel significant or important for the status and reputation it brings them, and they also feel love and connection for being part of their gang. They feel like being part of a family.

All their needs being met in one go also, but in a way that I hope you agree is wrong. Just like bullying—weak human behaviour.

The true football fan is using their club or team to fulfil their needs in a Win-Win situation.

The hooligans actually believe they are 'real' or 'proper' fans, that would die for their club, but it's false, and as big a con-trick as the bully.

The troublemakers are selfishly **using** that club as an excuse to get their human needs in a violent way. A true Win-Lose, that has been ruining the reputation of the sport for decades.

This can also be used as an example of why some of our youth fall for the con-trick of joining gangs.

Understanding these *emotional needs* will help you know the true 'WHY' behind any human behaviour or actions.

You will not get deflected by the 'story' of what happened, but instead you will know 'why' it happened, and that kind of understanding keeps you in control from the con-trick.

One of the reasons bullying has increased at an alarming rate (and now attracts people who would not have become a bully years ago) is the introduction of the internet and the smart phone.

I love the internet and smart phone, and I am in no way blaming them. They have helped us all in so many ways and are not to blame.

The blame lays 100% with weak human behaviour. No matter whatever has been invented, and introduced to people, there are always going to be some who will use it for selfish reasons to get their *emotional needs.*

Cyberbullying is one of the main contributors to teenage suicide, and the bullies are often anonymous, hiding behind a keyboard.

The cyberbully can attack anyone with insults, spreading false rumours, and even encouraging people to take their own lives.

Social media gives the bully an easy and weak way to satisfy their emotional needs, with no care for their victim.

Normal advice tells us to stay off the internet site, block the bully, or other avoidance advice. Although this is sound advice, it is easier said than done, and why should we have to anyway?

Why should we have to miss out in genuinely connecting with friends, and sharing with them? Nobody has the right to purposely make you feel hurt and upset, and that is why their weak behaviour needs exposing.

I have my opinions and my 'model of the world', but it does not give me the right to attack yours. The only reason that I would attack you is to get my emotional needs met. By using you to try and prove to myself (and everyone else) that my 'model of the world' is right and yours is wrong.

I am allowed to have my beliefs and think that I'm right, and I can share them if I want. But I do not have any right to attack you in anyway or comment nastily and directly to you.

This is just weak. And because you now know the true reasons driving the behaviour, it makes me look pathetic.

This is why we have to get the bullies to truly understand their weak behaviour. They must realise that we know the con-trick they are trying, and how pathetic their behaviour really is.

The bullies will not be able to get any response from us–anger or upset– so they won't get their negative *emotional needs* met.

Just remember that all they want is a reaction, and any reaction will do. When people give the logical advice of ignoring the bully, this is how you do it.

You first of all understand the weak emotional behaviour of a bully, and you don't provide them with any of their *emotional needs.*

There are so many examples and stories to explain this part of the book, but there are not enough pages to share them with you. Therefore, I will show you where you can get this explained in even more detail at the end of the book.

It only takes one of the examples to 'click' with your subconscious friend. Then you will get it, feel it, see it, and truly know it for certain.

Top Tips

When helping kids understand their *Emotional Needs* and the bullies' *needs*, use stories and examples that they can relate to. It may be a movie or programme they like to watch, or book they like to read. You can use examples of real-life experiences they have already had.

This obviously should be age appropriate, which is your decision.

The human emotional needs are present in everything if you take the time to really understand this chapter. Grasp it yourself first and then share it with your child, a little bit at a time, just like 2+2=4.

Once your child's subconscious friend has this information stored it is going to make all the difference. They will automatically see through any con-trick the bully wants to try.

If this is done by a teacher to the whole class, then the desired outcome is much quicker and so much more effective. When all the kids in the class understand the con-trick, any bullying will stand out to everyone as weak and pathetic. The bully will not get what they want.

If the whole school are taught the information, then this is when we make a real difference.

This will firstly help all the good children, and hopefully help the bully change their behaviour.

We cannot change anyone's behaviour for them; it must come from them.

Change will only come from better information and a reason for them to change.

Some mind notes for your conscious and subconscious friends.

- Everything we do or say is to fill our *emotional needs.*
- The bully is weak because they are simply **using** others to get their *needs* in a weak and selfish way.
- We don't have to know exactly which *needs* the bully is after.
- The bully doesn't really know which *needs* they are after, they just feel it, but don't understand their weakness.
- Bullying is never personal.

One more quick example of our *emotional needs.*

Did you know that I am getting all my *emotional needs* just by writing this book?

I have certainty that the information I am sharing will make a difference, because it already has for so many. I have some uncertainty (excitement/variety) because I don't know if you will use this information to help others or not.

I feel some significance/importance because I am the one writing and sharing the information to help others. And I feel a sense of connection with you reading this, as we both have a common concern about bullying.

Any of my *emotional needs* could have stopped me writing this book because of the fear of failure, rejection, or ridicule.

If I wasn't sure and certain, or I doubted this information, it could have stopped me. If the uncertainty of what you would think of my writing, or the fear of being judged, may have stopped me.

Maybe feeling less important, because you ridicule and criticise me, could have stopped me. Or even the feeling of not being liked or loved because of this book. The list goes on.

The point is that I am not in control of how you feel about anything to do with this book. Your opinion will be based on your model of the world and it is not personal to me.

It's time for me to get the kettle on and have a coffee. I will be putting the coffee powder in the cup first. Then I will add the boiling water, give it a bit of a stir, and finally add the milk.

My wife is a bit strange, as she has the coffee powder and the milk stirred in first–before the hot water! Can you believe that? But guess what? Because I do not try to force my 'model of the world' on her, I make my wife's coffee the way she likes it and we are both happy.

A little pattern interrupt there for your conscious mind, and a subliminal message for your unconscious/subconscious mind.

Sometimes people bully or ridicule others just because of different personalities. Let's get into the next chapter so I can explain more.

CHAPTER FIVE

PERSONALITIES – LEG 3

WHAT KIND OF personality do you have? Have you even thought about it?

There are many different training models of personality profiling, and if you work for a large company, chances are you may have had a training company use a program like D.I.S.C., to do a psychological profile of all the staff. This is usually to find out your strengths in leadership, teamwork, and other such areas.

I share a simple colour version that I learnt over twenty-five years ago. It is not aimed at you understanding your strengths in the workplace, but to simply understand & accept that as humans we have some personality differences (just like our models of the world).

People sometimes bully others simply because they have a different personality to their own. It's weird, I know, but hey that's emotions for you. Someone who is quite loud and confident may end up picking on, or bullying, someone who is a little quiet and reserved.

Or it could be the opposite. Someone who is quiet, ends up spreading rumours and hateful messages online of someone loud and confident, because they feel less significant than them. The examples are endless.

Some people with the same personalities will clash also, simply because of their emotional needs kicking in. Humans eh!

There are four main personality types, and this is the model I use to explain them.

RED – Leader – Decisive – Determined – Driven – Results Orientated – Strong Ego

BLUE – Outgoing – Influencing – Inspiring – People Person – Impulsive – Talkative – Persuasive

GREEN – Detail Orientated – Accurate – Careful – Cautious – Analytical – Likes To Get Things Right

YELLOW – Steady – Team Player – Stable – Supportive – Reliable – Dependable – Safe

There are statistics to provide the percentage of people in each of the four main personality types, but you don't need to know this information. We are keeping it simple.

As a simple generalisation, people develop a main personality type, along with a secondary type. Notice that I said develop. We are not born with a personality type, we develop them.

Have you ever been compared to a family member, maybe even a distant relation? Have you been told something like "You're just like Grandma Margaret, on your dad's side of the family"? It is not generic; it is simply a part of human behaviour.

The main reason that I share this information is to encourage kids not to judge others by their personalities, but to understand and respect our differences. To realise that there is no right or wrong personality–only right or wrong attitudes.

Can you see how this fits in with our model of the world (Leg 1)? Can you see how some people's emotional needs (Leg 2) might be affected by other people's personalities? All the parts of this human behaviour program fit in with each other.

It is all about educating and understanding simple human behaviour, so as to truly understand 'The Truth About Bullying'. This will then place us all in a stronger state to deal with the problem.

Another reason I share this 'leg' is to highlight that we should not believe that we are fixed to our main personality type. I like to call this being a chameleon—becoming adaptable to other personalities.

For instance, you may believe that you are not a Red-Leader, but I guarantee there will have been a time that will have had to be, or even chose to be. If you are a parent or a teacher, then you have had to be a leader with your children.

There will have been a time when you will have been a Blue-Influencer, also maybe the Green-Analyser, and been a Yellow-Team player.

I encourage children and adults to simply understand their own, and other peoples preferred personalities, and to become flexible enough to adapt and change their behaviour sometimes to fit into other people's personality type. This is a huge skill with people, that will serve them well in the future.

As I write this, I have found myself wondering about your 'model of the world', and your main 'Emotional Needs'. I wonder what your main personality is like.

If I could meet with you now, I would understand without judging you, and I would not have the need to judge or criticise you to others, in private or public.

This is what I want our children and youth to learn on a daily basis, so that it becomes as natural and certain as 2+2=4.

Right then my friend, now that we have a basic fundamental understanding of 'The Truth About Bullying', what do we do with it?

This is what 'Leg 4' is for. The magic equation to everything in life. The No.1 Success Principle in the whole wide world. The answer to all your problems. Have I built this up enough he he?

I love this part, so let's go.

CHAPTER SIX

E + R = O - LEG 4

WHEN I TRAINED with Jack Canfield in America, the first Success Principle he shared was E+R=O, which is Event + Response = Outcome.

He learnt this equation from a psychotherapist called Dr Robert Resnick, and it is used to take 100% responsibility for your life & results–good or bad.

I will explain it briefly and then show you how we will be using it with the bullying problem.

The basic idea is that if you do not like the outcomes (O) you experience in life, there are two choices you can make.

The first choice (which most people do) is to blame the event (E) for your outcomes/results (O). A simple example is that I am feeling down and fed up because of the rainy weather, and I am blaming the weather (E) for how I am feeling (O).

I start saying to myself "It's the weathers fault that I'm feeling down, and it's put me in a bad mood for the rest of the day"

As well as blaming the weather, I am also blaming the council, the government, my parents, my kids, my wife, my old teachers, and the next door neighbours dog's uncles gold fish from three years ago, for all my failures and limiting factors to my happiness & success.

Most people place the blame for everything, including their bad feelings, on outside events and circumstances.

Here is the thing. We cannot control the weather. The weather does not have any feelings—it doesn't think to itself that it will put Norry in a bad mood for the day! It is just the weather, and it is what it is. Yet, I choose to give it the power over my emotion and feelings (see where I am going with this).

The second choice we have is–instead of blaming the event (E), we change our responses (R) to the events (E)—the way things are—until we get the outcomes (O) we want.

We cannot control the weather, but we can control how we respond to it. We are in control of our thoughts, what we picture & visualise in our minds, and our actions (behaviours). That is it—the three things we're in control of—nothing else.

Once we truly realise this, then we have the power and ability to respond (R) to ANY life events (E) and change our outcomes (O).

There are literally millions of different examples to explain E+R=O fully, and if you want to learn more then check out jackcanfield.com for details.

I use E+R=O for EVERYTHING in my life, and I can honestly tell you with 100% certainty that it makes a difference.

I have shared E+R=O with a few thousand people in trainings, privately, and in online groups. Many of the breakthroughs that people have had have been amazing and life changing, once they truly understand it.

Using the principle of Event + Response = Outcome, we are going to change it to Bullying + Our Response = Our Outcome.

With all the information we now know about the con-trick behind bullying, we are in a better state to respond to the bullying problem to create the outcome we want.

Unconsciously (at the foundation level) the bully wants you in a state of anger or upset. If they see your outcome is emotional pain or anger, then their outcome is a win and their emotional needs are temporarily achieved in a weak & selfish way. But only if you respond in a way that gives them it!

You see, now that you know how the con-trick works, and you are now in control of how you respond, you are going to stop giving the bullies what they want.

If I call you stupid or ugly, you must respond and somehow agree in your mind (remember your 50'000 self-talk thoughts) for it to hurt and upset you (your outcome). It is not what Norry says to you—it is what you say to yourself that creates your upset or anger. A little tough love coaching here.

Look at these two simple examples of different responses.

Norry/Bully + Your Response = Your Outcome/Feelings

1. Norry calls you stupid and ugly. Your self-talk says "Why is he being so mean, that hurts me. Maybe I am stupid and ugly. Do other people think I'm ugly? Someone in class laughed at me and called me stupid when I got the wrong answer etc etc"

Your outcome is that you are now upset or angry, and your self-esteem & confidence takes a hit. You have fed my *emotional needs.*

2. Norry calls you stupid and ugly. Your self-talk response is "I know with certainty that Norry is calling me names to get his Emotional NEEDS. He is using name calling to deflect me away from the truth. He is trying to use me in a weak and selfish way. Norry is trying to steal my self-esteem & confidence like a con-trick. Anything Norry says to me is based on his model of the world, and driven by his *emotional needs,* and it is not personal to me. I am not falling for Norry's con-trick, and I am in control of my responses. I choose to respond by showing Norry that he cannot affect my outcomes and happiness"

Your outcome is now more positive, and you are in a better 'state' to deal with the bullying.

This is a simple example and I am not saying it is going to be easy at first. But with enough repetition like 2+2=4, it does work.

It means that we are now in a better 'state' to deal with the bullying. E+R=O does ***not*** mean that we have to put up with any form of bullying.

Most victims of bullying are scared of reporting it to adults or authorities in case it makes the bullying worse. But for the outcome to change we must encourage everyone to stand up to the weak bullying behaviour, by reporting these incidents without fear of being judged or retaliation.

This will only happen by educating all our school children repeatedly with The Truth About Bullying. Drip fed daily from parents and teachers, so that it becomes 100% certain in their conscious & subconscious mind. It will take some time, just like learning their times tables. But once they know it—it cannot be undone.

Once the bullies truly understand their behaviour, then they will have no excuses to use anymore, and will have to take responsibility for any outcomes/punishment they bring on themselves. It will also be their motivation to change their bullying behaviour.

It is going to take some work from parents & teachers, but it will be worth it. The alternative is to carry on with the same responses we have been doing and hope for the best. Unfortunately, the results show that those ways are not working, and that the bullying & mental health problem in children is getting worse.

I'm sorry, but this is not acceptable to me. And I hope by now you feel the same way. A different response (R) must be done, and this information will definitely help.

As I mentioned at the beginning of the book, this program is not meant to replace any of the other bullying programs and information already being used. It is designed to complement them and help give a stronger foundation to their message and outcomes.

When you look at a building, you see the structure and its cosmetics. What you don't see is the most important part of that building...... it's foundation.

If the foundation has not been done right, then no matter how well the rest of the building has been built, it will eventually weaken and collapse. Let us get this foundation of 'The Truth About Bullying' into every child and every school and make a direct difference for our future generations.

CHAPTER SEVEN

YOUR RESPONSE

LET ME GO first.

My response to the bullying problem is providing this book, a video course for parents, and 'The Truth About Bullying' training program for schoolteachers and staff with the help of The MADD Challenge.

MADD stands for Making A Direct Difference, and we are going to supply EVERY school in the UK (over 30'000) with FREE access to the trainings on bullying. If we train the teachers, then they can drip feed the information to our children and they will truly be making a direct difference to the bullying problem. This in turn will be helping with the mental health problem in our youth.

This is my response to the bullying problem and my main personal goal. This is my passion and it WILL get done.

What is your response going to be?

Are you going to take responsibility and read this book a few times to truly understand the bullying problem?

Is your response going to be to start drip feeding examples with your children?

Because there is so much more that I want to share with you, and I fear it may make this book too long to read and absorb, I have also put together a parents online training course with videos for you to access. These go into more detail and explain the other emotional needs along with what I call the 'magic triangle', which I believe is the best way for dealing with the bullying problem.

The videos will give you a better understanding of 'The Truth About Bullying' and you will have unlimited access to the information forever.

If you are reading this as an eBook then you can directly access the videos using this link–https://youthpotential.mykajabi.com/tab-book-course

If this is a physical book, you can go to youthpotential.mykajabi.com and get access to the videos.

As a parent & grandparent myself, I want to encourage you to re-read this book and take advantage of the video course. You can make a direct difference to your children's future.

I also want to personally ask you to tell other parents & teachers about this book anyway you can—social media will be a great way for you to share where they can get their copy of The Truth About Bullying.

Together we can reveal The Truth About Bullying… one parent at a time–one teacher at a time–one school at a time.

It starts right now with you!

—Love Norry x

For any further information, you can go to our Facebook page—Youth Potential—or email me at youthpotential@outlook.com

ALL THE MONEY RAISED FROM THIS BOOK WILL BE USED TO HELP SUPPLY SCHOOLS WITH THEIR FREE TEACHER TRAINING PROGRAM ON BULLYING.

Printed in Great Britain
by Amazon

50631428R00037